Facts About the Moose

By Lisa Strattin

© 2019 Lisa Strattin

FREE BOOK

FREE FOR ALL SUBSCRIBERS

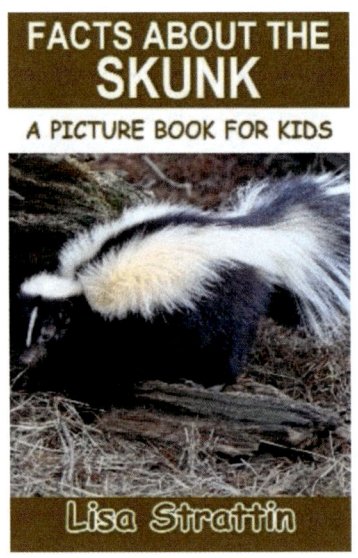

LisaStrattin.com/Subscribe-Here

BOX SET

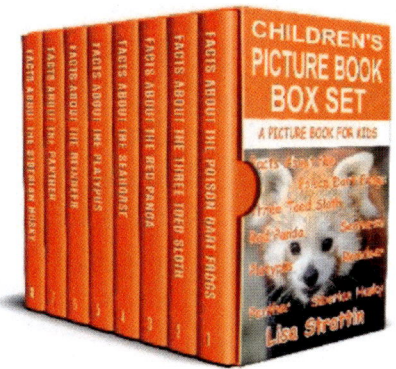

- **FACTS ABOUT THE POISON DART FROGS**
- **FACTS ABOUT THE THREE TOED SLOTH**
- **FACTS ABOUT THE RED PANDA**
- **FACTS ABOUT THE SEAHORSE**
- **FACTS ABOUT THE PLATYPUS**
- **FACTS ABOUT THE REINDEER**
- **FACTS ABOUT THE PANTHER**
- **FACTS ABOUT THE SIBERIAN HUSKY**

LisaStrattin.com/BookBundle

Facts for Kids Picture Books by Lisa Strattin

Little Blue Penguin, Vol 92

Chipmunk, Vol 5

Frilled Lizard, Vol 39

Blue and Gold Macaw, Vol 13

Poison Dart Frogs, Vol 50

Blue Tarantula, Vol 115

African Elephants, Vol 8

Amur Leopard, Vol 89

Sabre Tooth Tiger, Vol 167

Baboon, Vol 174

Sign Up for New Release Emails Here

LisaStrattin.com/subscribe-here

All rights reserved. No part of this book may be reproduced by any means whatsoever without the written permission from the author, except brief portions quoted for purpose of review.

All information in this book has been carefully researched and checked for factual accuracy. However, the author and publisher makes no warranty, express or implied, that the information contained herein is appropriate for every individual, situation or purpose and assume no responsibility for errors or omissions. The reader assumes the risk and full responsibility for all actions, and the author will not be held responsible for any loss or damage, whether consequential, incidental, special or otherwise, that may result from the information presented in this book.

All images are free for use or purchased from stock photo sites or royalty free for commercial use.

Some coloring pages might be of the general species due to lack of available images.

I have relied on my own observations as well as many different sources for this book and I have done my best to check facts and give credit where it is due. In the event that any material is used without proper permission, please contact me so that the oversight can be corrected.

COVER IMAGE

By USDA Forest Service - http://www.epa.gov/glnpo/image/viz_nat4.html, Public Domain, https://commons.wikimedia.org/w/index.php?curid=10561389

ADDITIONAL IMAGES

https://www.flickr.com/photos/apbutterfield/14595965832/

https://www.flickr.com/photos/alvaro_qc/2658215375/

https://www.flickr.com/photos/58122391@N03/5550701410/

https://www.flickr.com/photos/40263796@N05/8666439617/

https://www.flickr.com/photos/40970749@N06/7743167974/

https://www.flickr.com/photos/apbutterfield/14595965732/

https://www.flickr.com/photos/usfwshq/6862339335/

https://www.flickr.com/photos/denalinps/5302689686/

https://www.flickr.com/photos/jglitten/30398745688/

https://www.flickr.com/photos/larry1732/15007485110

Contents

INTRODUCTION 9

CHARACTERISTICS 11

APPEARANCE 13

REPRODUCTION 15

LIFE SPAN 17

SIZE 19

HABITAT 21

DIET 23

ENEMIES 25

SUITABILITY AS PETS 27

INTRODUCTION

There are thought to be six different subspecies of moose found in forests today. These are the European moose (found in Finland, Sweden and Norway), the Eastern moose (found in the eastern area of Canada and northeastern states of the United States), the Western moose (found in the western region of Canada), the Siberian moose (found in the eastern area of Siberia and Mongolia), the Alaska moose (found in Alaska and the Yukon) and the Shiras moose (found in Wyoming and Utah).

CHARACTERISTICS

The male moose have enormous antlers that renews once each year. After the warmer mating season the male will shed its antlers for the winter. In the springtime the moose begins to develop new antlers which take from 3 to 5 months to fully grow.

Although moose are not usually aggressive, when provoked, moose have been known to attack people. Although the injuries of a moose attack are generally minor, they have been known to attack more people than attacks by bears and wolves put together!

APPEARANCE

The moose has a long head with a large nose and upper lip. They have small ears, a small tail, and a dewlap (a loose fold of skin) hanging on their throat. They have powerful shoulder muscles that give them a humpbacked appearance. The male or bull moose has huge broad and flat antlers that can stretch 4 to 5 feet across from tip to tip.

REPRODUCTION

Female moose do not have antlers and tend to give birth to a baby moose after an 8 month gestation period. Pregnancy usually results in a single moose calf but twins and triplets have been known to occur on occasion.

The fur of the baby is a reddish color that turns to brown as it gets older. The young moose calves stay with the mother until just before the next young are born.

LIFE SPAN

Moose live until they are about 16 years old in herds.

SIZE

An adult moose can weigh up to 1,600 pounds!

HABITAT

The moose lives in forested areas where there is snow in the winter and there are nearby lakes, bogs, swamps, streams and ponds. The moose's large size makes survival in warm climates difficult, and they have trouble when temperatures rise higher than 80 degrees Fahrenheit.

In the summer, they cool off by stepping into the water that is in their native range.

DIET

Moose are herbivorous animals and spend their time looking for vegetation and branches to munch on.

ENEMIES

The moose have been hunted by humans for both trophies and for meat.

They are also prey to a number of large meat-eating animals which they encounter in their home range, such as bears, cougars and arctic wolves.

SUITABILITY AS PETS

The moose is not really suitable to be a pet. They are simply too big! Since they are not normally aggressive to people, you might be able to watch one if you live in area where they are. You can probably see them in your city zoo, if you want to watch them and you don't live in the same areas that they do.

COLOR ME

COLOR ME

COLOR ME

COLOR ME

COLOR ME

COLOR ME

COLOR ME

COLOR ME

COLOR ME

COLOR ME

Please leave me a review here:

LisaStrattin.com/Review-Vol-275

For more Kindle Downloads Visit Lisa Strattin Author Page on Amazon Author Central

amazon.com/author/lisastrattin

To see upcoming titles, visit my website at LisaStrattin.com– most books available on Kindle!

LisaStrattin.com

FREE BOOK

FOR ALL SUBSCRIBERS – SIGN UP NOW

LisaStrattin.com/Subscribe-Here

LisaStrattin.com/Facebook

LisaStrattin.com/Youtube

Made in the USA
Las Vegas, NV
31 March 2022